HOLIDAYS *for the* HURTING
25 DEVOTIONS TO HELP YOU HEAL

HOLIDAYS *for the* HURTING
25 DEVOTIONS TO HELP YOU HEAL

ELISABETH KLEIN

REDEMPTION
PRESS

Cover design by Jacquie Walker of Jacqueline Walker Photography

Published by Redemption Press, PO Box 427, Enumclaw, Washington 98022, toll free (844) 2REDEEM (273-3336)

Redemption Press is honored to present this title in partnership with the author. The views expressed or implied in this work are those of the author. Redemption Press provides our imprint seal representing design excellence, creative content, and high quality production.

ISBN 13: 978-1-63232-758-1

Library of Congress Catalog Card Number: 2015948844

Sweet one,

I have walked through maybe a dozen painful holiday seasons over the course of my life. While other people excitedly bought presents and baked cookies and opened up their homes, I was doing everything I could just to stay above water.

The holidays are interesting. It's as if we feel we have to be more "on." That we have to enjoy life and our family more deeply. That we must do more and be more all the while still fulfilling our normal obligations, but with mysteriously some-how more joy and energy and time and money (that we don't have).

If you picked up this book, it's because you are going through something this holiday season that is making life a little bit harder, that is making you sigh a little bit more, and I'm guessing you are hoping to find within these pages a different kind of connection to Christ and the Christmas story.

You've come to the right place. Your life does not have to be perfect – or even close to it – to have a meaningful holiday season, to deeply experience the love of the baby Jesus turned Savior. He will meet you where you are, even in your season of sadness or pain.

Welcome to Holidays for the Hurting.

Elisabeth

Now in the sixth month the angel Gabriel was sent by God to a city of Galilee named Nazareth, to a virgin betrothed to a man whose name was Joseph, of the house of David. The virgin's name was Mary. And having come in, the angel said to her, "Rejoice, highly favored one, the Lord is with you; blessed are you among women!" But when she saw him, she was troubled at his saying, and considered what manner of greeting this was. Then the angel said to her, "Do not be afraid, Mary, for you have found favor with God. And behold, you will conceive in your womb and bring forth a Son, and shall call His name JESUS. He will be great, and will be called the Son of the Highest; and the Lord God will give Him the throne of His father David. And He will reign over the house of Jacob forever, and of His kingdom there will be no end." Then Mary said to the angel, "How can this be, since I do not know a man?" And the angel answered and said to her, "The Holy Spirit will come upon you, and the power of the Highest will overshadow you; therefore, also, that Holy One who is to be born will be called the Son of God. Now indeed, Elizabeth your relative has also conceived a son in her old age; and this is now the sixth month for her who was called barren. For with God nothing will be impossible." Then Mary said, "Behold the maidservant of the Lord! Let it be to me according to your word." And the angel departed from her.

Now Mary arose in those days and went into the hill country with haste, to a city of Judah, and entered the house of Zacharias and greeted Elizabeth. And it happened, when Elizabeth heard the greeting of Mary, that the babe leaped in her womb; and Elizabeth was filled with the Holy Spirit. Then she spoke out with a loud voice and said, "Blessed are you among women, and blessed is the fruit of your womb! But why is this granted to me, that the mother of my Lord should come to me? For indeed, as soon as the voice of your greeting sounded in my ears, the babe leaped in my womb for joy. Blessed is she who believed, for there will be a fulfillment of those things which were told her from the Lord."

And Mary said:
"My soul magnifies the Lord,
And my spirit has rejoiced in God my Savior.
For He has regarded the lowly state of His maidservant;
For behold, henceforth all generations will call me blessed.
For He who is mighty has done great things for me,
And holy is His name.

And His mercy is on those who fear Him
From generation to generation.
He has shown strength with His arm;
He has scattered the proud in the imagination of their
hearts.
He has put down the mighty from their thrones,
And exalted the lowly.
He has filled the hungry with good things,
And the rich He has sent away empty.
He has helped His servant Israel,
In remembrance of His mercy,
As He spoke to our fathers,
To Abraham and to his seed forever."
And Mary remained with her about three months, and
returned to her house.

(Luke 1:26-56 NKJV)

Contents

ANGER

I picture being in Mary's shoes. I'm young. I'm engaged to a good man. My life is planned out. I know my lot and my place in the world. And then an angel comes to me and tells me that I will become pregnant because the Holy Spirit will come upon me. And Mary handles this with the grace and calm and wisdom of not just a woman older than her years but a woman who is practically otherworldly.

And I think though how I would've handled this:

I think it's safe to say that I would not have been so accepting.

I think it's safe to say that I would have had my doubts.

I think it's safe to say that I would have been scared. Really scared.

And I think it's safe to say, sadly, that I would have been angry. Angry that my sweet little life I had planned out was not going to go the way I had thought.

I have had many of those moments. When I've looked around my life, when I have sat with the reality of who I was and where I was and the people who were around me and how my choices had shaped me, I was not always pleased with what I saw.

I have been angry with people in my life.

I have been angry with myself.

And I have been angry, if I'm completely honest, with God for either allowing certain circumstances or causing them to come to pass.

And perhaps this is you today. Christmas is just up ahead. You are supposed to be celebratory.

And yet, maybe you have just gotten a diagnosis that changes everything.

Maybe one of your children has placed distance between you in any manner of ways.

Maybe your spouse has died or left you or told you he's leaving you or is currently being unfaithful or abusive or floundering in an addiction.

Maybe you hate your job. Maybe you just lost your job. Maybe you can't find a job.

It could be anything. Anything at all that doesn't line up with the life you had hoped for or at the very least had assumed you would be living.

And today, with the holidays approaching, you are angry. At someone. At yourself. At life. At God.

You might be angry with God just as you're supposed to be acting like you're super happy to be celebrating the gift of his Son's arrival.

Today as I write, I'm angry about something. I'm upset with God for taking something away. And my anger isn't going to dissipate just because "it's coming on Christmas."

We are allowed our anger, just like any human emotion. But what we do with it is what matters. So today, sweet one, I suggest you lay it out before God. He can handle it.

Be angry and do not sin. (Eph. 4:26a NKJV)

God, I come to you angry. You know why I am. But I don't want to become a bitter person, especially during this season. So I am giving it to you. Please meet me in this pain. Please teach me and heal me and help me choose kindness. Amen.

Broken

No one wants to feel broken at Christmas. But you do. We want brokenness to stop for holidays and special events, but life just isn't like that. So here you are. You are moving slowly. You are hurting. You feel listless, painfully aware of what's not right in your life or in your heart.

And then there's Christmas. With the lights and the gifts and the baking and the dreaded Christmas letter (how do you sum up where you are right now in that darn family Christmas letter?! Ahh, maybe this is the year you don't write one).

How can you and your brokenness coalesce with the Christmas season? You don't want to do Christmas. You want to stay in bed until January 2nd-ish.

Here's how.

You tell God – who sent Jesus as a baby and who holds your circumstances in his hands – how you feel.

You lay it all out before him. You tell him you feel broken. You tell him you're done. You tell him you've had it up to here. You tell him that Christmas, this year, will just have to go on without you.

You roll it all onto him, as my mentor says. And then you wait. And you rest. And you take a look at your holiday to-do list and maybe scratch out a thing or two (no one will miss that letter).

You just let yourself be broken.

Do not for one moment think that you need to be something you're not. That you need to muster up wholeness and fake-happy just because it's December.

You do not.

And if you think you do, who told you that?

If it's anyone other than Jesus, you do not have to listen.

You, sweet one, just walk your broken self to that Baby in the manger. You kneel down. You tell him you love him and tell him you're broken and you ask for his healing and love. That's all you have to do today.

That's all.

The Lord will perfect that which concerns me. (Ps. 138:8 NKJV)

God, I am hurting. I can't see past my pain today. I do not want to celebrate Christmas. I'm sorry, but it's true. I need you to heal me. I need you to carry me. I just need you. Amen.

Doubt

My life, right in this moment, is not where I want it to be. A promising part of my future has ended and my heart is aching. And because of that I am doubting a few things.

In my confusion, I am doubting my perceptions of reality.

In the surprise of this ending, I am doubting that my future is really merry and bright.

In my sadness, I am doubting the rightness of God's plan.

And I can't help but wonder if Mary had twinges of doubt. I know that pretty much right away she said to Gabriel, "Let it be to me according to your word," and I know that she has been hailed as being a young woman of great faith, but still. She was just a girl. And she was only human. And she knew what it was supposed to take to make a baby.

I do not want to diminish her faith. It is remarkable. It is to be lauded. It is to be replicated.

But I cannot help but ponder if she doubted anything in those moments . . .

Will this really happen to me?

Is this really the best plan for my life?

What is God thinking?

All questions you and I have probably asked ourselves at some point. Some of which we might be asking right now in the middle of our hurting season.

I feel like doubting gets a bad rap. But perhaps doubting isn't even the right word. *Questioning? Wondering* maybe?

We're allowed to do those things. I do not think, especially in our pain, that we are expected as mere humans, to just move forward blindly without using our minds and hearts to wrestle through our pain.

So today as you look to Christmas – the coming of the Lord – and you are hurting and waiting and wondering, know that it's okay.

It's okay if things feel off.

It's okay if you don't know what to think.

It's okay if you have more questions than answers today.

You do not need all the answers.

God is a great big God. He can handle the questions. He isn't afraid of your ponderings. I believe he understands how hard times throw us off kilter. Maybe today is all about being okay with not knowing and not seeing clearly and not understanding. Maybe that is the gift you can give yourself today.

God is not the author of confusion but of peace. (1 Cor. 14:33 NKJV)

God, I am confused by my circumstances. Nothing is clear. Nothing seems right. I can't see your hand in any of this right now. So today I ask that you help me simply accept my reality for what it is and sense your peace. Amen.

ENOUGH

I am not sure what your particular pain is today. It could be anything. Life is just so hard. Mine, right now as I write, is the ending of something sweet that has left me feeling a little bit not enough.

However, I remember a trial several years back when a false accusation swept into my life. That trial was the hardest and longest of my life up to that point. And though I kept trying to press into Jesus, I remember feeling like I wasn't godly enough to handle it.

I wonder if that's you today.

I wonder if you're questioning your ability to handle your hard situation.

I wonder if you're feeling like you are not enough of a woman to love your husband well. Or not enough of a woman to keep your husband around. Or enough of a woman to attract a husband in the first place.

I wonder if you're doubting if you're a good enough employee, mother, friend, daughter, *anything*.

I wonder, even, if you feel like you are not enough of fill-in-the-blank to create a meaningful Christmas experience for your family in the midst of your pain.

Enough-ness. Not a word, but I think it should be.

For whatever reason, I believe women walk through their lives not feeling like they are enough of anything.

But what I want you to hear from me right now – and I'm whispering this to my own soul – is this:

We are enough.

I am enough.

You are enough.

I believe God sent his Son to us for this reason, among many others: to show you that just as you are, he would love you and come for you. You were enough for him to leave heaven and join us here and search you out and then give his life for you.

He didn't do this when you were amazing. He didn't do this because of your sinlessness. He did this before his love took over your heart.

Which must mean one thing: even more so – with his life coursing through your veins – *you are enough.*

God demonstrates his own love for us in this: While we were still sinners, Christ died for us. (Rom. 5:8)

God, I feel like I'm letting you and everyone around me down. I feel like I don't have what it takes to get through this day let alone this season. I don't feel enough. But you say that I am. Help me believe it and live it. Amen.

EXHAUSTION

Are you tired today, sweet one? Can you maybe not see rest anywhere on your horizon? Does your hard thing appear endless to you right now?

And in the middle of all of it, it is Christmastime. And you are supposed to do an extra thousand things that you don't normally have to do.

You are tired.

You are weary.

You are carrying the weight of the world on your shoulders.

You want to stay in bed.

You do not want to face the world.

You are *exhausted*.

I have one word for you today:

Rest.

That's it. No big sermons. No huge principles from Scripture.

Just *rest*, sweet girl.

Lie down.

Close your eyes.

Take a nap.

Make a cup of tea.

Take in some deep breaths.

Read a magazine.

Watch a movie.

Go to bed early.

Rest.

And Baby Jesus grew up to say, *"Come to me, all you who are weary and burdened, and I will give you rest."* (Matt. 11:28)

God, I am so tired. I am so done with this trial, with this pain, with my life. I am weary. This is me . . . coming to you . . . asking for your rest. Please. Amen.

Expectations

Expectations are a slippery slope. Expecting anything other than the mighty, beautiful, mysterious, sometimes painful but always good will of God to unfold in your life is dangerous.

And yet, we do this all the time.

I'm sure Mary expected her life to go one way, and then an angel told her of a sharp turn it would be making. But I also wonder what kind of expectations she placed on her son-Savior?

Did she expect extra help from God the Father in her mothering?

Did she expect Joseph to have no struggles in loving this boy?

Did she expect her son to be well behaved all the time? (Was he?)

Did she expect Jesus to love her even more than the typical boy with his typical mother?

Did she expect him to live a full, long life?

What did Mary have to lay down? What crosses did she have to bear?

What expectations are you holding onto today, my friend?

Did you expect that God would have come through for you by now?

Did you expect that pain wouldn't wrap around you all day every day?

Did you expect this holiday season would surely be different from last year or the year before or the year before that?

Did you expect that by now you would've been healed? Or at the very least felt some peace?

What are you grasping onto?

What expectations do you need to lay down today?

Hand them over. It may hurt. You may feel powerless. But, honey, you already are. And that's the best possible place to find yourself.

As the heavens are higher than the earth, so are my ways higher than your ways and my thoughts than your thoughts. (Isa. 55:9)

God, today I am filled with unmet expectations. I thought this would be over by now. I thought I would have seen you moving. I thought you would protect me from something like this. Please help me see my situation through your eyes. And please help me lay down every single expectation that is boxing you in. I'm not fully there yet but help me want your will for my life, not mine. Amen.

FEAR

I've been reading the first two chapters of the Gospel of Luke this month as I prepare my heart for Christmas. And I found something that has surprised me. In the one hundred and thirty-two verses of those two chapters, an angel tells three different main characters not to be afraid.

He tells Zechariah not to fear because *his prayer has been heard.*

He tells Mary not to fear because *God has a surprise for her* (quite the understatement, don't you think?).

And he tells the shepherds not to fear because *he's here to announce a great and joyful event.*

I think I underestimate the part that fear plays in my life. I think I wrongly consider myself to not be a fearful person. But in essence, I think I fear quite a bit. What might happen tomorrow. What might not happen tomorrow. That I might have a sadness hover just under the surface of every experience for the rest of my life. That I might make hugely wrong decisions. That I might mess up my kids profoundly. That I might be missing what God's purpose is for me. You know, little things like that. But what I'm seeing from Scripture as I look at Luke's account of the arrival of Jesus is the common theme of not fearing – of being told to not be afraid – as if it's something we supposedly can choose to do, because it must be.

My head knows every single thing about worry and fear that there is to know:

That it doesn't add even an hour to my life.

That it isn't this proactive barrier that will make the potential bad news easier to bear.

That it takes my mind off the present.

That it's basically saying I don't believe that there is a loving God guiding my life.

I know, I know, I know. I know all of these things. And, for the most part, these truths do make their way to my heart and reside there.

There is a reason, I'm sure, that Jesus says *do not be afraid* like a zillion times. I think it's because, in part, he knows our tendency to jump to fear as our default reaction. But I think it's also because he knows something that we keep failing to truly integrate into our lives.

That his Father, who is also my Father, really loves me. That our Father is not out to get us. That he's not coming up with wild schemes to mess with our heads and leave us feeling untended and abandoned. That anything that comes our way – and I really mean *anything* – has been lovingly sifted through his hand before it enters our lives.

Author Ann Voskamp says in her book *One Thousand Gifts* that "all fear is but the notion that God's love ends." My life is proclaiming with each catch of my breath from worry that deep down I believe God's love for me can come to a stop. If only, in those slivers of moments just between a worry emerging and my entire body responding to that worry, I could remind myself that 1 John 4:8 says that *God is love*, which means he cannot stop being something that he fundamentally is, nor can he stop acting in accordance with his character.

So today, this is how I'm choosing to prepare my heart for Christ. I will lay down my fears for this day. I will set aside my dread and place it in my Father's capable hands. I will ask Jesus to help me be courageous by way of resting my weary mind in the hopes that space will be cleared for sweeter, truer thoughts to fill my soul.

35

"You have nothing to fear. God has a surprise for you." (Luke 1:30 MSG)

God, I am scared. My life is scaring me right now. I need you in new ways to enter into these places of fear. Please come. Amen.

Forgiveness

The holidays typically mean that you will be spending time with extended family. And perhaps you're in a place where a family member has hurt you, or even is currently hurting you. Maybe just the thought of Christmas Eve dinner with someone makes you nauseous because of the pain they have caused you.

Might I suggest something that you might not want to hear?

This might be the perfect time to offer forgiveness as the best Christmas gift you could ever give.

A few reminders:

Forgiveness is not the same as condoning.

Forgiveness is not about the other person; it is about you and your heart.

Forgiveness takes one person; reconciliation takes two.

You are only responsible for yourself and your thoughts and your words and your actions. No one else's.

Forgiveness can set you free.

Unforgiveness is deceiving. It makes you feel like you're in control, like you're a better person than the offender. When in actuality, unforgiveness is a trap that keeps you in places you don't want to be.

Has someone in your family hurt you?

Are you holding on to that pain?

Are you dreading your family get-together because of it?

It's time, sweet one. It's time to let this go. It's time to forgive. It's time to move on. It won't be easy, oh no. It will be one of the most difficult things you do.

But I believe Jesus came to set the captives free. Let him set you free from unforgiveness this holiday season.

"The Spirit of the Lord is on me, because he has anointed me to proclaim good news to the poor. He has sent me to proclaim freedom for the prisoners and recovery of sight for the blind, to set the oppressed free . . ." (Luke 4:18)

God, you know that I am holding onto unforgiveness right now. You see into my heart. You see the damage it's doing, the toll it's taking. I don't want to be a bitter person. Today I choose to forgive. Help me see this through. Amen.

GOODBYES

Christmas, in a good year, feels like one great big *hello* to me. The ultimate introduction. The best ever person has come into the world.

But you may be facing this holiday carrying only memories, hearing only *goodbyes*.

It could be from a miscarriage.

A house you love going on the market.

A husband who has left you or whom you have left.

A husband or family member or friend who has passed away.

Or even a dream that has died and the door is firmly closed with no hope of reopening.

And the last thing you want to do is say *hello* to anyone or anything new. Your life is shrouded in goodbyes.

I'm not going to ask you to set aside your grieving for the sake of the holidays. I wouldn't dream of suggesting you simply press pause in your pain. Life doesn't work like that. A heart cannot function that way.

But I would like to point out this one simple truth in the midst of your painful farewell.

Though every person in your life you will either have to say goodbye to at some point or they will have to say goodbye to you, and though some dreams just aren't meant to come to pass, you will never, and I mean never, have to say goodbye to Jesus.

He is the only hello that will never need to be followed up at some point with a goodbye.

So move closer into him today. Our sweet Baby Jesus is coming . . . and he's staying. He's here.

He Himself has said, "I will never leave you nor forsake you." (Heb. 13:5b NKJV)

God, I am grieving. I have said goodbye before I was ready. I need your comfort. I need your strength. I need your healing. And I need to believe in new ways that I will never have to say goodbye to you. Amen.

HEALING

ealing is perhaps one of my absolute favorite words. It calms me. It soothes me. It gives me hope.

But maybe even more than that . . . it reminds me that if there is a healing, then there is a Healer.

That we have a Healer.

That I have a Healer.

That you have a Healer.

Jesus came for a multitude of reasons and theologians might argue that some are more important than others.

He came to die for our sins.

He came to kill sin and death.

He came to teach us how to live life correctly or better.

He came to make us more like him.

He came to bridge the gap between God and man.

He came so that we could go to heaven.

He came to teach us how to love.

And all of this is true. And yet there's so much more.

But one of the best reasons, in my humble opinion, that Jesus came for us is this:

"The Spirit of the Lord is upon me because he has . . . sent me to heal the brokenhearted . . ." *(Luke 4:18)*

He came to heal those of us who are brokenhearted.

I am among the brokenhearted.

And if you are reading this today, then I'm going to not-so-boldly assume that you are among the brokenhearted as well. And that you are in need of healing.

Listen, I have walked through deep waters and passed through the fires. And I can tell you that time did not heal me. And my friends, whom I love, did not heal me. And books, God love 'em, did not heal me. And counseling did not heal me. And the Church did not heal me.

If I have ever been healed – and I have, time and time again – it is because Jesus is my Healer and Jesus bent low and came close to bring me healing.

And as you lean in to Christmas, as it's coming closer and closer, I want to invite you to ask sweet Baby

Jesus to bring you the healing you so desperately need. And then believe and wait in expectation.

Have mercy on me, O Lord, for I am weak; O Lord, heal me, for my bones are troubled. (Ps. 6:2 NKJV)

God, there are broken parts of me right now. I am choosing to believe that when you say you sent Jesus to heal the brokenhearted, you meant me. Come, Lord Jesus, heal. Amen.

HOPE

Hope is a tricky concept. If, in the middle of your difficult season, you are pinning your hopes on your circumstances turning around, I would gently caution you.

There are no guarantees in this life.

No one has promised us anything.

Well, that's not true exactly.

Our sweet Baby Jesus grew up to promise us this: "In this world you will have trouble . . ." (*John 16:33a*).

What you're going through right now – the pain that you are carrying today – was promised to you.

If you have grown up under the false belief that life were supposed to be easy, I am so sorry. Life is hard. Life is complicated. Life is painful. In this world, we *will* have trouble.

But we *do* have hope.

Because Jesus went on to say: "But take heart! I have overcome the world" *(John 16:33b)*.

Our hope is not to be found in a shifting circumstance that rolls back our way.

Our hope is found in Christ alone. In the knowledge that he has overcome the world. In the trust that he is holding us. With the faith that he knows what he's doing.

Our hope does not disappoint, because our true hope is God himself. Shift your eyes to that manger and breathe out a prayer of thanks. He came for you, to bring you hope.

Hope does not disappoint, because the love of God has been poured out within our hearts through the Holy Spirit who was given to us (Rom. 5:5 NASB)

God, my hope has been misplaced. I have been hoping and praying and wishing that you'd turn things around. Instead, my hope and focus should be on you alone. Help me look to you. Please come be my Hope. Amen.

HURTS

I'm thinking about Joseph today. What a good man
he was. How he planned to take Mary as his wife
and take care of her and provide for her. How he
probably hoped for children, for a son. And the pain
he must have felt when he found out Mary was with
child. And that it wasn't his. And even the confusion
that came after the dream when the angel told him to
take Mary as his wife as planned. That must've hurt.
His life was changed on him, without his permission.

How much of your life has been changed on you
without your permission?

How many other people have made choices that
have affected you negatively?

How has even God swirled things around in such a
way that you don't even recognize your life anymore?

Is this you today?

Are you hurting at the hand of someone else? Or yes, we can say it, Someone else?

I am today. I didn't see it coming. I wasn't prepared. And there's nothing I can do to change the new circumstance.

It's one thing when we do something that hurts ourselves. We can learn and grow and try to change and prevent the same thing from happening again. But when someone else hurts us, it leaves us on shaky ground, feeling vulnerable and exposed. And it may leave us feeling out of control, powerless.

(Here's a little secret: We *are* out of control. We *are* powerless.)

And it's in those moments when we have an opportunity. Like Joseph had an opportunity to divorce Mary quietly and move on or lean into this difficult, unexpected situation. And we know what he chose. He chose the difficult. He chose the uphill battle. He chose to walk through his sadness and not run from it.

Let me encourage you to open yourself up to Jesus in a new way. Enter into your pain. Ask him to join you in it. Acknowledge who has hurt you. Admit that you feel out of control. Sit with the fact that someone has hurt you and you feel raw. It's okay.

It's really okay to be honest about your pain. It's even really okay to put a name to your pain if it truly were another person who has hurt you. Even at Christmas. Even when it's inconvenient. Even when you'd rather just live in denial.

So here's what we do when someone hurts us:

We grieve the loss.

We accept our new reality.

We walk out our lives under some sadness until the sadness fades.

(And at some point, if necessary, we choose forgiveness.)

We're moving closer to Christmas. And you are hurting. And someone may have done something to you. And it's left you unmoored. But Jesus is coming. *And* Jesus is here, even in your pain.

Jesus said, *"You'll be sad, very sad, but your sadness will develop into gladness."* (John 16:20b MSG)

God, you know I've been hurt and you know who did it. I need you to walk me through my sadness. I want to learn from it. I don't want to run from it or gloss over it just because it's Christmas. Please come closer. Amen.

JOY

I did not want to write today when I saw that the next topic on my list was *joy*. In fact, I closed the document and went on to do some other tasks and even went for a walk. Anything not to have to write about joy today. Because I am not feeling joyful.

And then I realized, neither are you, more than likely. So perhaps, when I don't feel joy is the perfect time to write about joy.

Because joy is not a feeling.

Joy is not based on a circumstance.

Joy is not the same as happiness.

Joy is a choice.

Joy can come in the middle of pain.

Joy can come in the middle of sadness.

Joy can come in the middle of weariness.

Joy comes in the morning.

Today I am sad and confused. I am struggling to see hope in my future. I so wish this weren't the case. I wish I were steadier in all things no matter what was going on around me. But this is my reality.

And today, I'm wondering what you are feeling, dear reader? Are you sad? Confused? Is hope evading you? Are your circumstances swirling? Are you unsteady?

Then these are the circumstances in which you are best able to lean into Jesus, which sets the foundation for joy seeping into your soul.

I am a believer that joy comes from gratitude. So in the midst of your painful situation right now, I want you to pause and thank Jesus for every single good thing in your life that you can think of, big and little. Nothing is too small to thank him for. He is our good-gift provider. I'll start you off . . .

Jesus left heaven for you.

Jesus was born of a virgin for you.

Jesus lived a spotless life for you.

Jesus died on the cross for you.

Jesus came back to life for you.

Jesus hears you.

Jesus sees you.

Jesus holds you.

Jesus created you.

Jesus plans to redeem your pain.

Jesus loves you.

Jesus . . . (Keep going, sweet one . . . what else has Jesus done for you?)

Weeping may last through the night, but joy comes with the morning. (Ps. 30:5 NLT)

God, I am lacking joy today. But since you command it, it must be a choice. So today, I thank you for all of your goodness and faithfulness and intimate care. Help me choose joy in my pain. Help me lean into you. Amen.

Loneliness

I'm thinking of Mary, deciding to visit Elizabeth. The text does not say that she brought Joseph with her. The distance, if walking between Nazareth and Judah, was twenty-two hours. She would have been young, pregnant, perhaps alone. Though she carried the Savior of the world within her and though she believed in God, I can only imagine the loneliness that sweet young girl must've felt as she traveled.

And I'm wondering, if in the midst of your hurting season, are you lonely too?

There is something about dark nights of the soul that drive us inward. You can reach out all you want, but when it truly comes down to it, it is just you and Jesus.

There is something about that that is unsettling. And something about it is beautiful. There is something about it I want to turn from. And then there is something about it I want to embrace.

Hard times leave us scrambling to feel better. But our usual tricks just don't work during these seasons. Our friends can try to come near, and we're grateful, but in the quiet, there is a deep loneliness that accompanies our confusion and sadness.

Today, if you are lonely as you look to the arrival of the Baby Jesus, know this: his mother more than likely was too as she waited for him. And yet, she kept walking, kept obeying, kept praising.

My soul magnifies the Lord, and my spirit has rejoiced in God my Savior. (Luke 1:46-47 NKJV)

God, I feel so alone. I feel so lonely. I carry this emptiness with me and though I've asked you to fill it, it remains. Please meet me in those empty places. Please teach me to sit with the longing as I wait for you. Amen.

Perseverance

Most of my heart-shaping, life-defining trials were not quick. They lasted for a season. Sometimes they have lasted for years, decades even.

Sometimes, life feels like walking a very long way in the same direction without knowing how long you'll be walking or quite where you're headed.

That takes faith. And it takes perseverance.

Again, I think of Mary. She was mothering the Savior but she did not know to what end. She poured her heart and life out, I imagine, as mothers tend to do. And she couldn't see how her story and her Son's story were going to play out.

Are you walking in a story that you cannot see the end of?

Is it driving you a bit mad?

I am. There are currently two areas of my life that are confounding me. One is my work. I have put my hand to the plow, I am not looking back, and I am giving everything I've got to this desire to help hurting women by bringing them hope, in every way I can think of. And yet, I have no idea if this will take off, so to speak. If I will be able to support myself. And it's scary to me.

And then there's my singlehood. I had just gotten used to being single again when a new relationship formed and then ended and then I found myself back, not at square one, but back to having to sit with my reality that I in fact may be alone for the rest of my life, humanly speaking, partner-wise.

And yet, I must keep walking. I must keep showing up at my laptop every morning and keep doing my work. And I must keep getting out of bed and showing up at my life every morning and keep, well, living it. All without knowing the outcomes. I must persevere.

And so must you. Like Mary, we do not know how things are going to turn out. But like Mary, we are called to be faithful; we are called to obedience. We are called to keep walking and moving forward. Even in our pain. Even in our uncertainty. Even when we want to give up.

Consider it pure joy, my brothers and sisters, whenever you face trials of many kinds, because you know that the testing of your faith produces perseverance. Let perseverance finish its work so that you may be mature and complete, not lacking anything. (James 1:2-4)

God, I want to quit. My life. My job. My marriage. My parenting. This trial. All of it. I'm done. I don't have it in me to move through this day. (Deep breath.) But I won't. I will keep walking. But I desperately need your help. Jesus, please give me your strength to get through this one day in front of me. Amen.

RAW

I know of a woman whose beloved dog died the day after her wedding. Life is funny like that. Every day, we gratefully hold in one hand joys and blessings that are immeasurable, and in the other hand, we begrudgingly hold life's deep hurts and blinding disappointments.

Life does not wait for good timing to bring something our way.

And Christmas is no exception. You may have just entered into a season of pain as the holidays started up. And the newness of the situation has left you not just unsettled and unmoored, but raw.

You are raw in that you do not know how to process what has swept into your life. Or you might be raw in that this thing – whatever your thing is – has rubbed you down to your core. It's like wearing new shoes for a long day of walking and you can feel with every step that skin is being removed.

Or like me, you find yourself raw because an old issue that you thought was either worked through or healed or at the very least buried down deep enough to be a non-issue has resurfaced, and it hurts, and it's uncomfortable, and you do not know what to do with it.

We cannot fix ourselves. We cannot heal ourselves. We want to because we don't like to feel unpleasant things and because we like to think we're in control. But we cannot.

I think of Mary in those very first moments after the angel left her, before she told anyone of the news of her pregnancy. She must have felt stripped bare. She must have been beyond confused. She must have been in awe. She must have been raw.

And yet, bless her heart, her kneejerk reaction was to submit in obedience.

"Let it be to me according to your word," she said.

In her rawness, she obeyed. In her rawness, she laid down her dreams for her life. In her rawness, she turned her heart to God.

Let the bones you have crushed rejoice. (Ps. 51:8)

God, I am without a way to heal myself today. I cannot take away my own pain. I am bare before you, I am weak, I am raw. I need you. Please cover me and heal me. Amen.

REJECTION

This is one of my least favorite words in the English language: *rejection*. It dredges up old wounds of abandonment and being the one left, the one not chosen, the one cast aside.

I wonder if Mary felt rejected when she heard these words being spoken by her grown Son:

> *Then His mother and brothers came to Him, and could not approach Him because of the crowd. And it was told Him by some, who said, "Your mother and Your brothers are standing outside, desiring to see You." But He answered and said to them, "My mother and My brothers are these who hear the word of God and do it."*
> *(Luke 8:19-21 NKJV)*

If you have gone through a break-up, or your husband is choosing an addiction or another woman over you, or you are separated or divorced, or you have been fired or passed over for a promotion, you know the sting of rejection.

Is this you today?

Has someone looked into your eyes and said, with their actions, *I do not choose you?*

I know, sweet one. I know. I am all too familiar with that pain.

My consolation is that I have a Savior who came to earth for me.

Who loves me.

Who says I'm precious and honored in his sight.

Who says I am enough.

Who sings songs of delight over me.

Which means . . .

Baby Jesus came to earth for you.

And he loves you.

And he says you are precious and honored in his sight.

And he says that you are enough.

And he sings songs of delight over you.

And he will not forsake us, he will never abandon us, he will not reject us.

Be strong and courageous. Do not be afraid or terrified because of them, for the LORD your God goes

with you; he will never leave you nor forsake you.
(Deut. 31:6)

God, I feel rejected. By this person I trusted and loved. And maybe, if I'm really honest, by you for letting this happen. Please meet me in this feeling of abandonment and aloneness. I need to feel you and experience you, especially in the midst of the busyness and chaos of this season. Come near. Amen.

Sadness

I went through a period of feeling lost. Sad. Blah. Passion-less. I purchased a book to help me work through the sad state I was in and I was clipping right along. I did everything it told me to do: I came up with a life timeline, listed the negative points, processed the redemption that has come from each, and decided upon my five primary roles. This was all good and fine; I felt like I was accomplishing something.

And then . . . and then I hit a wall.

So I did what I usually do when I hit a wall: I spent some time with my mentor. And I was telling her about this process that I was making myself go through and how, when I got to the step where it asked what my ambitions were – how I wanted to live out my life in each of my five roles – how I hit a wall and couldn't think of anything to write down under any of them, after thinking and praying about it for several days.

I told her that for the past twenty years, I've had various passions. Mothering young children, then women's ministry, then social justice. That I'd poured myself into each of these things, wrote about these things, been an advocate for these things. But that right then, I didn't have a passion for anything.

And she said, "I have your answer."

"Okay," I said. "What is it?"

And then she said something like this, "Years ago, when people lost someone they loved, it was expected that they would mourn for a year. They were given black arm bands to wear. They even put black wreathes on their front doors. They were to rest and grieve and heal. They even had places in the middle of their town called Melancholy Park where they would be allowed to go and just sit. Can you imagine? No one would bother them, no one made fun of them, no one pushed them to get back into their regular lives. They were not only allowed but encouraged to do the grieving work, for a year."

I sat there, tears streaming down my face, not even four months past my divorce at the time.

She continued, "You have lost something big. Picture yourself with a black arm band. Let yourself rest. Let yourself grieve. Let yourself heal. I'll let you know if I think you're not doing enough. But right now, just rest. Because if you don't do the work now, it'll come out eventually."

I went home and put that book away. The process of finding my new place, my next chapter, my next thing, would wait a few months. (Okay, many months.) Because in that moment, I had the deeper work of rest to accomplish. How I wished I could live in Melancholy Park. (She says we can only visit . . .)

Is this you this Christmastime? Do you need permission to visit Melancholy Park? You have it. I'm giving it to you. Go rest and be sad.

The LORD is close to the brokenhearted; he rescues those whose spirits are crushed. (Ps. 34:18 NLT)

God, I am sad. Sadness is hanging over me like a cloak that is too heavy for me to wear. Please meet me in Melancholy Park. Please help me not feel guilty for feeling this way. Please help me walk through it with your grace and mercy. Amen.

STRESS

Life is hard. We are all stressed. Someone on Facebook posted that he overheard an eight-year-old say to her mom, "I'm so stressed out. What are you going to do about that?"

Now whether she was just parroting what she's heard her parents say or she truly is a frazzled eight-year-old, either way is both sad and scary.

And then enter Christmastime. When everyone's expectations of each other and ourselves go through the roof, on top of all of our regular responsibilities, and no matter what sadness or pain we find ourselves walking through.

Stress upon stress upon stress.

So today, I'm going to ask you to rest. That is your task today. To look at your mounting to-do list and scratch one thing off. You heard me. Just simply eliminate something. Don't move it to tomorrow or next week or January. Just take it off the list.

And in that space created by not doing that one thing, I want you to stop. Do not fill it up with doing another thing. Just stop. Lie down and take a nap. Or sit on your couch, maybe with a cup of tea or coffee or hot chocolate. And do nothing. For like, fifteen minutes . . . thirty if you're feeling daring. Yep.

In the middle of your day. In the middle of your life. In the middle of your Christmas. In the middle of your difficult season. In the middle of your stress.

Do. Nothing. (Even if it kills you.) (Hint: *it won't kill you.*)

You are tired. You are carrying heavy burdens. You are carrying things you were never meant to carry. Jesus came for so many reasons but one really beautiful one is to lighten your load. Look towards Christmas morning. Today, as you sit doing nothing, rest in the thought that he wants to carry your burden *and* carry you.

"Are you tired? Worn out? Burned out on religion? Come to me. Get away with me and you'll recover your life. I'll show you how to take a real rest. Walk with me and work with me—watch how I do it. Learn the unforced rhythms of grace. I won't lay anything heavy or ill-fitting

on you. Keep company with me and you'll learn to live freely and lightly." (Matt. 11:29-30 MSG)

God, I am so bogged down by the details of life, by the pain and stressors of my life. I can't keep going. Meet me in this place of rest. Help me recover my life. Help me hand over my burden to you. Please carry it for me. Please carry me today. Please help me live my life freely and lightly. Amen.

Suffering

Today I think of Mary, but not as the expectant or new mother. As the mother of our Savior who stands by watching her son on the cross. I'm not sure I can fully imagine the level of suffering she must have endured in those moments.

Though I have yet to experience that type of suffering, I have suffered in this little life of mine. And you have too. And you more than likely are right now.

Suffering does something to us. It shapes us. It breaks our hearts. It softens our souls. If we're yielded to God, it reaps the rewards of helping us become a more grace-filled, gentle person. If we're not yielded, it can do untold damage.

It's Christmastime. You are suffering. It might feel like something small to you or to others who look into your life. It might be something from your past and most people wouldn't even know you're still suffering under the weight of it or they would think you should just be over it by now, whatever *it* is. Or you could be smack dab in the middle of a pain that you have no idea how you're going to get through.

But it's Christmastime. And we are all supposed to be happy-happy about the new Baby King that's coming. And you're not. You are weighted down under your silent – or not-so-silent – suffering.

It's okay. It's all okay.

You don't have to pretend to feel something you're not, no matter what anybody says. You don't have to muster up fake joy because it's the holidays. If you're suffering, sit with it. Don't beat yourself up. Don't try to talk yourself into happy. Just be.

Today, let the Baby who came at Christmastime who then grew up to be your Savior sit with you in your suffering today. He suffered, he understands suffering.

For we do not have a high priest who is unable to empathize with our weaknesses. . . . (Heb. 4:15)

God, my heart is breaking under the burden of the pain in my life. I cannot even muster up a fake smile today. Please come sit with me in my pain. Please bring me rest. Please help me know I'm not alone and that you understand. Please be my Shepherd. Amen.

TRUST

We've established by now that life is hard and unfair and full of unexpected surprises, and that it does not care if it's the holidays when it drops something into our lives that sends us reeling.

But here is something I have learned about hard times: *God is sovereign and to be trusted.*

About ten years ago, I was absolutely convinced that our family should adopt a little girl from Africa. I begged God. I begged my then-husband. I told God, as scared as I was to pray this, that I would take my then-husband's answer as God's answer. The answer came back *no*. A *no* that sent me reeling. And I felt the Spirit impress something upon my heart that I have never forgotten. I felt him say as clear as day, "If you think this man can thwart my plan for you, you are giving him too much credit and me not enough." Bam.

And I can apply that statement to any life scenario just as easily. And you can apply that statement to your life as well.

Are you in the middle of a pain that just does not make sense to you? What is your unanswered question today? What are you walking through that seems murky and non-understandable? A recent, abrupt job loss? A recent marriage ending that doesn't make sense? A recent death that came too soon?

Are you, like me, able to pull back just a little bit from the pain of the moment, from the details of the situation, and take a broader view and trust . . .

. . . that, even in your pain, perhaps God is working.

. . . that, even in your pain, perhaps he knows what he's doing.

. . . that, even in your pain, perhaps he is protecting you.

. . . that, even in your pain, perhaps he is preparing you.

. . . that, even in your pain, perhaps he is providing for you.

. . . that, even in your pain, perhaps he is making a way.

. . . that, even in your pain, perhaps something new and beautiful just may come from this.

. . . and that, even in your pain, perhaps he loves you completely and wants you whole and holy and free and is doing what he knows is best for you.

Can we, just for today, rest in a trust in the God who lovingly and knowingly sent Jesus to us? Today, just for today if that's all you've got in you, let's trust.

Fearless now, I trust in God. (Ps. 56:1 MSG)

God, I am having a hard time trusting in you today. Everything is so murky. But I want to. I want to believe that you are good and that you see me and that your hand is on my circumstances and on my life. Amen.

Unknowns

My eighteen-year-old daughter said to me, "I just wish I could know how my life is going to turn out."

I totally get it. I've got a few things myself that I'd give just about anything to get a little glimpse into the future on.

Maybe today you feel the same way. Maybe your pain has left you a bit numb, or you've stopped hoping for your future, or you are just downright scared of how some things might unfold before you. I know, sweet one. I know.

But I was thinking back on the past twenty-five years of my life, back to when I was my daughter's age, and I skimmed over the highlights and lowlights and realized that had someone told me what was coming back then, I would have been in a corner somewhere in the fetal position rocking back and forth.

I think God knew very well what he was doing when he decided not to give us the ability of seeing into our futures. I think having just the one day in front of us that we can make out is about all we can handle as humans.

Our minds and our hearts could not handle all of that foreknowledge at one time.

So that means today, we sit with the reality that we have no idea how any single part of our lives is going to play out. This can be very frightening. Or . . .

Or we can hold onto the Truth of the bigger story.

That the Baby who came from heaven to earth holds all of our lives and our hearts in his hand.

And that he is in control.

And that he knows what he's doing.

And that he will never leave us nor forsake us.

And that his plan for us is good.

And that he came to dwell among us.

And that he came to be our Counselor.

And that he loves us completely.

And that though we don't know how next year, or next month, or even tomorrow may go, we know that Jesus came. And we know that Jesus took on our sin. And we know that Jesus died. And we know that he rose again. And we can trust that the bigger story ends very, very well . . . us together with him who came at Christmastime.

For unto us a Child is born, unto us a Son is given; and the government will be upon His shoulder. And His name will be called Wonderful, Counselor, Mighty God, Everlasting Father, Prince of Peace. (Isa. 9:6 NKJV)

God, I can't picture how this dark season is going to end. I'm scared of the unknowns. Part of me wishes you'd whisper the outcome to me but the other part of me is choosing today to trust in your care and in your love. Amen.

VULNERABLE

There is something about going through a difficult time that makes me feel unprotected, uncovered. It's sort of like the emotional version of how I felt in the days following 9/11 . . . where I sort of sprinted to my car as if a plane would fall out of the sky at any moment.

I feel vulnerable during a hard stretch. I sometimes feel like God has perhaps turned his head and forgotten me.

I sometimes feel *unseen*.

I cannot imagine a more vulnerable situation than what Mary found herself in . . . young, unmarried, pregnant . . . oh, and with *God's child*. Scared. Lonely. No one in the world, literally, would be able to identify with her. So, so vulnerable.

And yet in her pain and fear and vulnerability, she obeyed God with a grateful and willing heart and she reached out to a friend.

Are you feeling vulnerable today? Forgotten? Unseen?

Are you feeling like God has up and left you to fend for yourself?

Like Mary, can you honestly say, even in your pain and fear and vulnerability, are you obeying God, gratefully, willingly?

And like Mary, even though I'm sure she felt no one would really be able to fully understand what she was going through, have you reached out to anyone who can walk with you through this season?

Those are my two gentle suggestions for you today. Come to God with a *yes*, as Mary did. And move toward a friend with your fear, as Mary did.

Then Mary said, "Behold the maidservant of the Lord! Let it be to me according to your word." (Luke 1:38 NKJV)

[Elizabeth] spoke out with a loud voice and said, "Blessed are you among women, and blessed is the fruit of your womb! (Luke 1:42 NKJV)

God, I feel unwatched-over right now. But I know you are here with me and I trust that you see me. Please do not leave me unprotected. Please fill me with your peace and your comfort. Please help me be grateful, willing and obedient. And please bring support around me. Amen.

WAITING

It's occurred to me that Christmas is a waiting season. But not just Christmas time . . . that *all of our lives* is just one big waiting season after another. Whether we're waiting on test results or acceptance letters or a marriage proposal or a loved one to peacefully pass away after a long battle. Or whether we're in a job we don't love and we're trying to figure out our next step. Or we've got five colleges to choose from and we can't tell which one to go to. Or we're in a hard marriage and we don't know if it'll ever get better. Or we're going through a divorce and don't know if we'll ever feel normal again. Or we're just hurting. And we want to feel just a little bit happy again. And we don't know if we ever will or when it'll kick in or if this is our lot.

We are all waiting. We are a waiting people, we humans.

And we have a choice: *we can wait poorly* or *we can wait well.*

Waiting *poorly* might look something like this:

Complaining. To everyone. All the time. Day after day.

Or conversely, *holding in* your feelings so your irritability comes out inappropriately on unsuspecting victims.

Stopping praying because it feels pointless or because you're upset with God.

Obsessing on whatever the thing is you're waiting on, becoming self-absorbed.

But waiting *well* looks like this:

Praying. Committing your desire to God, believing that he will give you the desires of your heart if they line up with his character and will for you.

Surrendering. I told Jesus that I felt lost today. That the waiting and unknowing were hard for me. But then I asked him what he wanted to teach me in the waiting and I asked him to help me wait well. I was super honest though, totally crying through my prayers.

Expressing. Get your feelings out. Share them with someone: a mentor, a best friend, a counselor.

Gratitude. Every day you have something to be thankful for. Every single day. Your life, your health, your breath, your home, your family, your friends, your God. So thank him.

Living. Listen, sometimes bad news requires an intertim of grieving. I totally get that. Yes, stay in bed for a day. Yes, cry your eyes out. Yes, punch a pillow. But then, sweet ones, we must keep living our lives, even in the murky. Even in the swirly panic. Even in the waiting and the unknowns. So as we say in recovery, do the next right thing when you don't know what else to do. Do what your day and life need you to do.

Waiting is hard. Waiting is part of life. Every person is waiting for SOMETHING. You cannot avoid waiting. But you can decide how you will wait.

Today, ask yourself: am I waiting poorly in my pain, or am I waiting well?

Wait on the Lord; be of good courage, and He shall strengthen your heart. (Ps. 27:14 NKJV)

God, I don't want to be an impatient person, a poor wait-er. Please teach me what you want me to learn in this waiting season. Please help me wait well. Please help me wait on you. Amen.

ARRIVAL

Oh, sweet one, it's finally here. *He* is finally here. We may have trudged through this holiday season, limping emotionally, dragging baggage and pain and fear and unknowns.

We may have put up the tree, we may have written the family letter, we may have bought everyone and their uncle presents.

Or we maybe have not. Maybe we did Christmas differently this year. Either out of necessity because a crisis came roaring into our lives or out of weariness because we just couldn't add another thing to our plates. Or perhaps out of choice, because we realized that moving a bit more slowly and not taking all those extra tasks on was what our hearts needed this holiday.

But we are here. This is the day when we sit with the realization that God came for us. Came to be with us. Came to win our hearts. Came to show us that we matter. Came to prove that he knows who we are. Came to crash through our pain and fear. Came to bend down even closer to us in our brokenhearted state.

He came for us.
He came for you.

In your anger.
He came for you.

In your sin.
He came for you.

In your disappointment.
He came for you.

In your fear.
He came for you.

In your pain.
He came for you.

To bring you healing.
To make you well.
To make you whole.
To comfort you.
To set you free.
To be with you.

Emmanuel, God with us. He is here. In the midst. He has arrived.

When all is said and done, the last word is Immanuel— **God-With-Us.** *(Isa. 8:9* MSG*)*

God, I am so very glad you came. Thank you for coming for me, to be with me, to walk me through my pain, to heal me. I need you. I receive you. I love you. Amen.

Additional Resources

World Split Open (Redemption Press, 2014)
Unraveling: Hanging Onto Faith Through the End of a Christian Marriage (Abingdon, 2013)
Surviving in a Difficult Christian Marriage (Amazon, 2014)
Living through a Divorce as a Chrstian Woman (Amazon, 2014)
Moving on as a Christian Single Mom (Amazon, 2014)

BLOG	http://www.elisabethklein.com/blog/
WEBSITE	http://www.elisabethklein.com
TWITTER	https://twitter.com/_elisabethklein
FACEBOOK	https://www.facebook.com/elisabethkleinwriter
PINTEREST	http://www.pinterest.com/elisabethklein1/
EMAIL	elisabeth@elisabethklein.com

An Invitation

In the summer of 2012, Elisabeth began two private Facebook groups: one for women who are in difficult Christian marriages, living out the day-to-day with their spouses; and one for Christian women who are separated or divorced, no longer living with their spouses. She now also moderates groups for women who are reconciling with their husbands, those who are single moms, and a group for women who are simply walking through a season of pain. If you are interested in being a part of any of these growing private communities, where the women are committed to following God and encouraging each other in their difficult circumstances, please email her at elisabeth@elisabethklein.com and she will gladly add you.

Biography

Elisabeth is wife to Richard and mom to teenagers, Sara and Jack. She gratefully attends Orchard Community Church in Aurora, Illinois. She began and led the Women's Ministry for ten years at her former church. She writes a monthly mothering column, and she writes regularly for websites such as Crosswalk, Grace for Moms, The Life of a Single Mom, and People of the Second Chance. She speaks a few times a month to women's groups. She is honored to be a member of

Redbud Writers' Guild. Her idea of a great weekend would include time with her husband and kids, time with her best friends, a bike ride, and some reading.

Testimonials

When I stumbled onto Elisabeth's writings, I remember thinking "I'm not alone! Someone gets what I'm going through and is living to write about it!" Her blog and books have been like a dear friend I could turn to for encouragement and understanding while God stitched my heart and restored my marriage. – *Angela*

I have drawn so much strength from her writings. You feel as though you are finally with someone who gets it – someone who can hold your hand and say, "I've been there, I've felt that, and I made it to the other side – you'll get there too and I'll be right here with you on the journey." – *Carolyn*

Elisabeth's work has helped me by letting me know I am not alone in feeling the hundreds of emotions I have while going through the separation and divorce process. – *Heather*

If you would like to support Elisabeth as she helps hurting women by bringing them hope, you can find more information here: www.patreon.com/elisabethklein

Contact Information

REDEMPTION
PRESS

To order additional copies of this book, please visit
www.redemption-press.com.
Also available on Amazon.com and BarnesandNoble.com
Or by calling toll free 1-844-2REDEEM.

CPSIA information can be obtained
at www.ICGtesting.com
Printed in the USA
FSOW02n2145251116
27836FS